The Story of
CAR ENGINEE
SOICHIRO HONDA

by **Mark Weston**

with illustrations by **Katie Yamasaki**
Additional material by **Pam Watts**

DISCARD

Lee & Low Books Inc.
New York

Text from *Honda: The Boy Who Dreamed of Cars* copyright © 2008 by Mark Weston

Sidebar text by Pam Watts copyright © 2018 by Lee & Low Books Inc.

Illustrations from *Honda: The Boy Who Dreamed of Cars*
copyright © 2008 by Katie Yamasaki

Photo credits:
p. 12 public domain
p. 13 Shutterstock.com
p. 19 Richard McDowell / Alamy Stock Photo
p. 21 David Kilpatrick / Alamy Stock Photo
p. 24 US Office of War Information / public domain
p. 26 Pictorial Press Ltd / Alamy Stock Photo
p. 33 public domain
p. 39 Universal Images Group North America LLC / Alamy Stock Photo
p. 43 David Falconer for the Environmental Protection Agency / public domain
p. 47 AP/Wide World Photos

LEE & LOW BOOKS Inc., 95 Madison Avenue, New York, NY 10016
leeandlow.com

Edited by Louise May and Kandace Coston
Book design by Abhi Alwar and Charice Silverman
Book production by The Kids at Our House

Manufactured in the United States of America by Lake Book Manufacturing, Inc.

The text is set in Volkhorn.
The display font is set in Avenir.
The illustrations are rendered in acrylic on canvas.

10 9 8 7 6 5 4 3 2 1

First Edition
Cataloging-in-Publication Data is on file with the Library of Congress.
ISBN 978-1-62014-790-0

To my sister, Carol Weston, who also writes for children. Her help, from the first idea to the final draft, was invaluable. — M.W.

For Leo and Diane Dillon with so much love and gratitude — K.Y.

TABLE OF CONTENTS

CHAPTER ONE

THE BOY WHO DREAMED OF CARS

I n the small Japanese town of Tenryu, far below snowcapped Mount Fuji, Soichiro Honda was born on November 17, 1906. As a boy he loved to watch the boats in the town's harbor. He wondered how the boats worked and where they went, and he dreamed of ports beyond the horizon.

Soichiro's mother wove cloth. His father worked as a blacksmith, hammering molten iron into fishing hooks, shovels, and farming tools. The oldest of nine children, Soichiro liked to watch his father make these things.

HOKKAIDO

JAPAN

HONSHU　Tokyo

SHIKOKU

KYUSHU　Tenryu

He also helped his father chop up big slabs of charcoal to stoke the fire in the blacksmith shop. The work was messy, and Soichiro was often covered with black charcoal dust.

One day when Soichiro was seven, a man drove a rumbling Ford Model T through town. Soichiro had never seen a car before. He ran beside it, amazed by the many moving parts. When he could run no farther, Soichiro crouched down and smeared his hands in a puddle of oil the car had left behind. He liked the smell. *Someday I will learn how a car works and make one myself,* he thought.

Soichiro was not a good student. Book learning did not make sense to him, but **machinery** did. When he was fifteen Soichiro moved to Tokyo, Japan's largest city. He found work in a garage where the owner, a **mechanic**, repaired American-made cars.

At first the garage owner was harsh. "Don't touch the cars, Soichiro," he said. "Your job is to sweep my garage and clean the tools. Nothing else. Do NOT touch the cars!"

Soichiro almost quit. "I want to learn how cars work," he muttered to himself. "I didn't come to this big city just to sweep a floor." But he decided to stay. He thought that if he kept the garage spotless, maybe the owner would be impressed and teach him to be a mechanic.

Day after day Soichiro swept the garage and cleaned the tools. He worked hard and did not complain. After he finished his assigned duties, Soichiro watched the garage owner work. When the mechanic let him, Soichiro handed him the tools the man needed while he repaired the cars.

The garage owner noticed Soichiro's dedication. After almost a year he finally told the boy he was a good worker. "Now I will show you how to make some basic repairs," he said.

Soichiro was thrilled. "*Domo arigato gozaimasu*," he said, bowing low. "Thank you very much."

"Domo arigato gozaimasu"
(Doh-mo ah-ree-ga-toh go-zy-mas)
Thank you very much.

Cars: A Brief History

Nearly every technological **innovation** is the solution to some problem. In 1900, the problem was horse manure. More and more people were moving to cities, and using horse-drawn carriages to get around. Experts at the time estimated that each horse produced about fifteen to thirty pounds of poop per day! The result was poop everywhere. And with the poop came flies. Flies carried diseases that made people very sick. It was an environmental and public health crisis.

People needed another way to get around that didn't require using horses. Many inventors experimented with the idea. Leonardo da Vinci designed the first known self-propelling vehicle in the early 1500s. But a practical alternative would use an engine and fuel to propel the vehicle instead.

There were a few possibilities. Steam engines were explored but never perfected. Electric engines were another early option. In 1900, the Electric Vehicle Company operated an entire fleet of battery-powered electric taxis in New York City. But most places didn't have electricity yet to charge the batteries, so battery-powered cars were impractical.

In 1886, a German **engineer** named Karl Benz introduced the first gasoline-fueled commercial automobile. It was called the Benz Patent-Motorwagen. It had only three wheels, was expensive to **manufacture**, and went just ten miles per hour (mph), so it didn't catch on—only twenty-five sold between 1886 and 1893. But it proved that gasoline-fueled automobiles were a **viable** alternative, and it paved the way for Henry Ford.

Henry Ford was the son of humble farmers near Detroit, Michigan. In 1891 he got a job as an engineer with the Edison Illuminating Company, run by Thomas Edison. In 1895, he saw an article about gasoline engines in a magazine. He was fascinated and decided to use one to make his own horseless carriage. The next year, he built his first vehicle. It was called the Quadricycle because, unlike the Benz Patent-Motorwagen, it had

Henry Ford sits in his first automobile, the Ford Quadricycle, 1896.

four wheels. Though it could go twenty miles per hour, it was a clunky machine. It had bicycle wheels, a **tiller** instead of a steering wheel, and no brakes at all. By 1903 Ford established the Ford Motor Company, and a few years later, he came out with the Model T.

A Ford Model T on display.

The Ford Model T revolutionized the world. It was quicker to produce than earlier cars, it could go as fast as forty-five mph, and it looked good doing it! It was sturdy enough for everyday travel and less expensive than most built-to-order cars of the day. It became the "workingman's Ford," and every workingman wanted one. Ford sold fifteen million Model T's worldwide over ten years. Best of all for big cities: the Model T finally solved the poop problem!

The Japanese began experimenting with cars in the early 1900s, but there was no market for automobiles in Japan. Most Japanese people at the time were poor farmers or laborers in large manufacturing and financial **conglomerates** known as *zaibatsu*, and thus few people could afford their own cars. However, the zaibatsu saw an opportunity to compete in the international automobile market. One of these zaibatsu, called Mitsubishi, made Japan's first mass-produced car, the Model-A, in 1917. But it wasn't until after **World War II** that Japan's automotive industry really began to thrive.

CHAPTER TWO
EXPERT REPAIRMAN

For six years Soichiro trained as a mechanic. He learned how to fix every part of a car. He rebuilt **carburetors**, which mix air with gasoline, and he replaced the spark plugs that **ignite** this **combustible** mixture to power the engine and get a car going. He adjusted brakes, patched tires, and put in new water pumps. He even fixed transmissions, the gears that turn cars' wheels and allow cars to speed up and slow down.

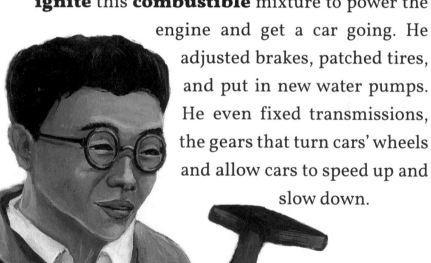

Soichiro was now an expert repairman, and he wanted to run his own shop. Tokyo already had many mechanics, so Soichiro moved to Hamamatsu, a city near his hometown.

It was a proud day for Soichiro Honda when he opened his garage in 1928. He quickly became known as the best auto mechanic around, and the mechanics in his shop repaired nearly every car in town. Within three years Honda had fifty employees working at his garage.

By the time he was in his late twenties, Honda had made a lot of money from his successful garage. He bought a house and

married a schoolteacher named Sachi. Soon they began to raise a family.

In his spare time Honda started designing race cars. He loved to drive fast, and in 1936 he built and drove the fastest race car in Japan. No sooner had Honda become the country's racing champion than he was seriously hurt in an accident. One of his brothers was also injured.

Honda's wife persuaded him to stop racing, but he still dreamed of making cars.

Street Racing in Japan

Almost as soon as the Japanese began to love cars, they started modifying them. The process of customizing cars is called *tuning*, and it involves changing parts of cars—the body, the engine, the tires, etc.—to make the car look cooler and drive faster for racing.

During Japan's period of economic and automotive growth after World War II, street race cars, called *hashiriya*, multiplied. Secret, illegal gangs organized to race on crowded highways and back roads. The most famous of these was called the Mid Night Club. They were like pirates of the streets. They defied the law in pursuit of the highest speeds, but they followed a rigid code of ethics while they did it.

The Mid Night Club started in 1987. In order to join, a person's *hashiriya* had to reach a speed of at least 160 mph. Japanese cars were legally built to go no more than 112 mph at the time, so Mid Night Riders had to be able to engineer their cars to go faster. Despite their fixation on speed, club members were bound by the rule that they would not put anyone else in danger with their driving. In 1999, a gang of motorcycle bikers, called *bosozoku*, decided to interfere with one of the Mid Night Club's races. The bikers forced the drivers into a high-traffic area and caused them to crash. Two bikers died, and two drivers and six civilians were hospitalized. The Mid Night Club disbanded immediately afterward.

The *Kanjozoku* are another infamous tuner gang. They race on the circuit of highway that surrounds the city of Osaka, and they drive only Honda Civics. They hide their identities by repainting their cars almost weekly and by putting nets in the windows.

All of these groups might have impressed Soichiro Honda, a lifelong racer himself. He even built his own racetrack—the Suzuka Circuit—to host international races. He believed that racing made his machines better—that it was the only way to perfect them.

A modern Honda Civic with gull-wing doors customized for racing.

CHAPTER THREE
THE HONDA MOTOR COMPANY

A year later Honda took an important step toward making his dream come true. He began manufacturing the metal rings that surround pistons. These small steel cups in a car's engine move up and down quickly inside cylinders as they convert the energy in gasoline into the force that turns a car's wheels.

Honda thought it would be easy to make piston rings, but his first ones were too rigid. They did not bend, and they cracked under stress. Ring after ring broke. So Honda went back to school to study metallurgy, the science of working with metal. Determined to figure out how to make his piston rings more flexible, Honda tried one technical approach after another. By 1940 his piston rings worked perfectly. He sold them to Toyota, one of Japan's first car companies.

This diagram from a motor manual shows the parts of a 1927 car engine and gearbox.

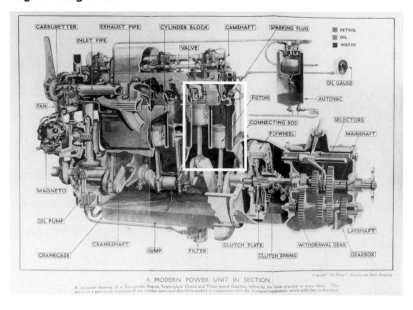

A MODERN POWER UNIT IN SECTION.

A CLOSER LOOK

The piston is a metal cylinder that moves up and down within the engine. When the piston moves up, it compresses the mixture of air and gasoline that's used to power the engine. A burst of flame from the spark plug ignites this mixture and pushes the piston back down. This quick downward motion rotates the crankshaft and helps drive the car forward.

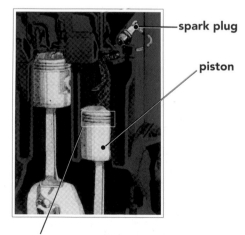

spark plug

piston

A piston ring creates a sliding barrier around the piston that prevents the gas/air mixture from leaking into the area beneath the engine.

In the early 1940s, during World War II, the Japanese air force asked Honda to make airplane propellers in addition to piston rings. When the war ended in 1945, Honda's propellers were no longer needed. Japan had been defeated. People could not afford to buy new cars, and car manufacturers did not need Honda's piston rings. Honda was discouraged, but he was able to make a living repairing old cars.

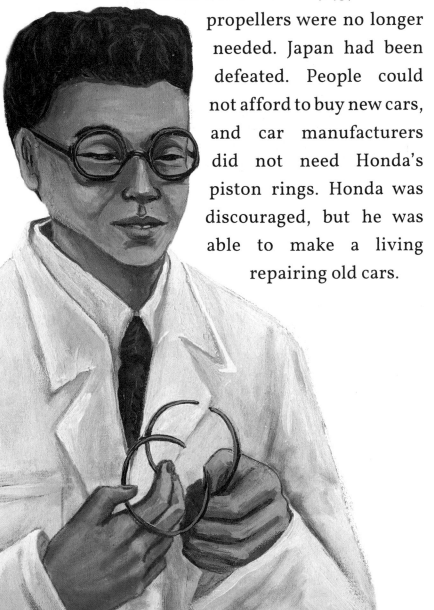

Japan in World War II

In the early 1900s, Japan sought to expand its power and boundaries. Its main target was China, and it invaded and occupied the region of Manchuria in 1931. But Japan's ambitions interfered with America's interests in Asia, so the US cut off Japan's access to oil and other key resources. To strengthen its hold on China, Japan secretly planned what was known as the Southern Operation to disable US and British naval facilities in the Pacific.

In 1940, Japan signed a pact with Germany and Italy, creating an alliance known as the Axis Powers. Germany was already at war with England and France, and the Axis powers agreed to help each other if any other country attacked one of them. The United States stayed out of the conflict until December 7, 1941, when the Japanese bombed the US naval base at Pearl Harbor in Hawaii as part of the Southern Operation. The attack killed over 2,400 people. The next day, the US declared war against Japan.

Although the US government had no proof, it suspected that Japanese Americans might be acting as spies for Japan. Two months after the bombing of Pearl Harbor, President Franklin D. Roosevelt signed **Executive** Order 9066, which effectively gave the military permission to arrest and imprison—without trial—all Japanese Americans living on the West Coast. Nearly one hundred and twenty thousand people were taken from their homes and communities and sent to prison camps surrounded by barbed wire, where they were forced to live the rest of the war. Many families were separated, many people died in the camps, and nearly all were subjected to extreme hardships, including inadequate housing and lack of medical care.

Japanese American children pledge allegiance in 1942.

World War II was the bloodiest conflict in modern history. The Nazis alone killed an estimated eighteen million people. Six million of them were Jews who died in concentration camps. The creation and use of the atomic bomb—a **nuclear** weapon—also contributed to the death count. Several months before the start of the war, a German chemist named Otto Hahn discovered that an **atom's nucleus** could be split to create energy. The **Allies** (comprised of the US, Great Britain, and the Soviet Union) feared that the Germans would use this discovery to build an atomic bomb capable of killing 100 times more people than any previous bomb. The Allies decided to build one first. They collected the brightest physicists currently in the US and built a town in the New Mexico desert, called Los Alamos, where they could live and work. The scientists began work in Los Alamos in March 1943.

On June 6, 1944—what is now known as D-Day— the Allies crossed the English Channel and landed in German-occupied Normandy in the north of France. It was one of the largest coastal military invasions in history, involving planes, boats, and ground troops. Though the Germans were caught by surprise and fought fiercely for eight more months, they were eventually defeated. Germany declared its **unconditional** surrender on May 7, 1945.

Despite its fallen ally, Japan refused to surrender unconditionally and grew more aggressive. It appeared that the United States would have to invade Japan to end the war. But in July, the scientists in New Mexico had tested the first atomic bomb in history, and on August 6, 1945, the US chose to drop one of these bombs on the Japanese city of Hiroshima. Japan did not immediately surrender, so three days later, the US dropped another atomic bomb on Nagasaki.

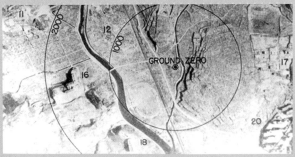

An aerial view of the city of Nagasaki before and after the dropping of the atomic bomb in August 1945.

It is difficult to give an exact estimate of how many people were killed by these bombs, because the aftermath of the detonations continued to affect people years later, but the total was close to 300,000. Most of the scientists who created the bomb felt deeply conflicted about what they had done. When Otto Hahn learned of the bombings of Hiroshima and Nagasaki, he wept.

Six days after the bomb was dropped on Nagasaki, Japan surrendered.

After the war, the US occupied Japan. The US authorities took all power out of the hands of the Japanese emperor and set up a democratic government. They broke apart the zaibatsu—Japan's large business conglomerates—and tried to create a fully **capitalist society**. These sudden changes led to an economic crisis in Japan, and it took many years to rebuild the economy. In 1951, Japan and the Allies signed a peace treaty, ending the occupation.

Gasoline was expensive after the war, so instead of driving to work, Honda often rode the train. He quickly grew tired of the crowded conditions, but the alternative—a bicycle—was too slow. Honda thought he could develop a faster bicycle. He added a tiny engine and a second chain belt, and turned a bicycle into a small motorcycle.

Honda converted five hundred bicycles into low-cost motorcycles. A local businessman, Takeo Fujisawa, was so impressed with these

new machines that he raised money to build a motorcycle factory. In 1948, the two men started the Honda Motor Company. Fujisawa liked Honda's down-to-earth personality and did not mind when Honda wore work clothes to business meetings. Honda appreciated Fujisawa's skills as a salesman and his ability to secure loans from banks when the company needed to borrow money.

Honda eagerly kept up with the latest

motorcycle technology because he wanted his motorcycles to be better than anyone else's. He figured out a way to double the power and gasoline **mileage** of his engines without making them more expensive. The small engines opened and shut like clamshells, which made it easy to reach the parts inside to make repairs.

Honda wanted all the motorcycles he made to be perfect. He often worked beside his employees on assembly lines and yelled at them when they

made mistakes. "We are not selling clothes. We are selling motorcycles," Honda would shout. "If we don't tighten a nut properly, we put the customer's life in danger." The factory workers started calling him Mr. Thunder, and they worked hard because they did not want to displease him.

Although Honda had a temper, he treated his employees fairly. He offered good salaries, and built company gyms and swimming pools. Honda called his workers "associates." He encouraged

them to share their ideas, and let them keep the money their inventions earned. "I have always had a stronger interest in the work than the money," Honda explained. He also created new jobs for associates when machines made their old jobs unnecessary.

Henry Ford and the Assembly Line

Henry Ford did more than build cars. He fundamentally changed the way cars and other goods were manufactured, ushering in the age of mass production. In order to make the Model T affordable for the masses, Ford knew he needed to decrease the cost of making the car and speed up production. He made many innovations to this end. But his most successful and important advance was in **standardizing** the use of the moving assembly line.

Before the assembly line, skilled laborers would build a part or the whole of a complex item, like a car. This took both training and time. In a moving assembly line, the building process is broken down into many simple actions. Each person on the line is only responsible for one of the actions. After a worker completes their actions, a conveyor belt brings the project to the next person. No worker needs to know how to do more than one small piece of the assembly, which speeds up production.

Ford did not invent the assembly line; elements of

it were already being used in meat-packaging plants and flour mills. But he combined these elements to create a successful system for mass-producing cars. Before the assembly line, it took fourteen hours to assemble just the body of a Model T. After the line went into effect, assembly took just an hour and a half. Because the Model T could be produced so quickly, the price of the car dropped from $850 ($20,000 today) to $290 (about $4,000 today).

Employees on the Ford assembly line in 1913.

Once automobiles were more affordable, people bought them in droves. The Model T was first manufactured in 1908, and around one hundred thousand were made in the first four years of production. In 1913 alone—the first year of the assembly line—Ford's Highland Park facility produced 170,211 Model Ts. Production increased nearly every year after that and finally peaked at just over two million cars in 1923. Around fifteen million Model T's had been sold by the year 1927. By then, America had become a country that drives.

CHAPTER FOUR
A NEW MARKET

By the late 1950s one third of Asia's motorcycles were Hondas. Now Honda had a new market to **conquer**. In 1959 the Honda Motor Company introduced its Super Cub motorcycles to the United States. Until then most Americans associated motorcycles with danger, loud noise, and gangs. But the Super Cub was too small to be scary. The advertising **slogan**, "You Meet the Nicest People on a Honda," projected an image of good, clean fun.

Sales soared as Americans who had never thought of riding motorcycles began buying them. Within five years the Honda Motor Company was making almost half of America's motorcycles.

In 1963 Honda returned to his lifelong dream of manufacturing cars. "I am not satisfied with being number one only in the motorcycle world," he told his associates. "Progress is when you go forward, when you keep graduating from one stage to another."

> "Progress is when you go forward, when you keep graduating from one stage to another."

For six years Honda made small cars just for Japan. Then in 1969 he decided to start shipping midsized cars to the United States. Before he did that he had to make a choice. Should the new cars have air-cooled or

water-cooled engines? Honda admired the German air-cooled Volkswagens. After much thought, he decided that his engines would be air-cooled too. "Who wants pumps and hoses and things that leak?" he said.

Tadashi Kume, a young engineer, was convinced that Honda's decision was a mistake. Kume felt nervous about disagreeing with his boss, but he knew it was important to be honest. "Water-cooled engines are quieter and more powerful," he told Honda. "If you want to build bigger cars in the future, you will have to switch to water-cooled engines."

Honda encouraged his associates to speak their minds, and he realized that Kume was right. Honda reversed his decision. The water-cooled engine Kume helped design had better gas mileage and cleaner exhaust than other engines.

How to Cool an Engine

In 1876, a German man named Nikolaus Otto patented the modern gasoline-fueled internal combustion engine. His basic design is still used in most cars today. The engine works by pumping a small amount of gas and air into a cylinder where it is lit on fire. This causes a mini-explosion, also known as combustion! The explosion gets translated into energy that moves the car forward.

Combustion occurs in the engine several thousand times per minute, which generates a lot of heat. But engines can be finicky, and if they get too hot, they won't run right. So they need to have a cooling system to keep them at the right temperature.

The simplest cooling system is an air-cooling system. In this system, the engine is designed with fins that direct air toward the cylinder when the car is in motion. The air passes over the cylinder, cooling it. Some designs also incorporate a fan that blows on the engine. And some engines even send the hot air into the passenger cabin to warm the riders in cold weather!

Air-cooling systems are simple and relatively light,

which can be important when designing a car, but they have a big drawback. If the air outside the engine is really hot or really cold, the engine will be too. So air-cooled engines can fail in extreme weather.

Water cooling solves that problem because liquid stays a constant temperature for a longer amount of time. In most water-cooling systems, spaces are built around the cylinder for water to flow through. The water circulates around the engine, cooling it down. When the water gets too hot, it is sent to the radiator at the front of the car. Air flows into the water in the radiator, reducing its temperature in turn. Then the water can be used to cool the engine again.

Today some motorcycles use air-cooled engines, but very few cars do.

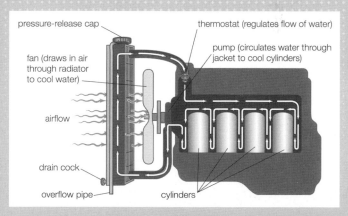

In this diagram of a water-cooled jet engine combustion chamber, arrows show how water circulates to cool the cylinders.

The new engine had a long name: the Compound Vortex Controlled Combustion engine. Its initials, CVCC, were the inspiration for the name of the first Honda car sold throughout the United States: the Civic.

The Honda Civic arrived in the United States in 1973. The timing was just right. Civics were the first car to meet the stricter **emissions**

standards of the Clean Air Act passed by Congress. When the price of gasoline **quadrupled** in 1973, Americans started looking for cars that made better use of the expensive gas. On highways, Honda Civics got more than twice the mileage of most American cars. Sales of Honda cars in the United States skyrocketed.

The Clean Air Act and the Energy Crisis

Two events in the early 1970s completely redefined the direction of the American automotive industry: the adoption of the Clean Air Act in 1970, and the oil crisis in 1973. During the 1960s, people in the US became more aware of pollution—air pollution in particular. Many US cities heavily involved in manufacturing were enveloped in clouds of **smog**. To address this issue, in 1970, the Clean Air Act was signed into law.

The Clean Air Act regulated the amount of air pollution across the country. Because cars caused a large amount of air pollution, the auto industry was forced to redesign their vehicles so that they **emitted** fewer pollutants. This was a big setback for the American automotive industry because American cars were known for being large, comfortable, and powerful—all qualities that caused higher emissions.

Around the same time, the US experienced an energy crisis. At the end of World War II, Britain withdrew from many of its colonies in the Middle East, and the nation of Israel was created as a Jewish state.

The new nation included most of the territory called Palestine, but the Arabs who already lived in Palestine did not want to give up their land. This sparked a conflict in the Middle East.

The US supported Israel in the conflict, but in the late 1960s, the Arabs realized they had **leverage** against the US. Most of the oil that the US used came from the Middle East, so the Arab members of the Organization of Petroleum Exporting Countries (OPEC) placed an **embargo** on oil shipments to the US. Oil suddenly became scarce, and as a result, the price of gasoline in America quadrupled. To keep costs down, Americans wanted to buy smaller, more fuel-efficient cars. Together, the Clean Air Act and the embargo shifted the US automobile market away from the large, gas-guzzling, luxurious cars that the US was known for and toward

the small, light, energy-efficient cars that Japan had quietly been perfecting for years.

Gasoline shortages hit the US in 1973.

CHAPTER FIVE

HONDA'S LEGACY

In 1973, when Honda was sixty-six, he retired as president of the Honda Motor Company. He thought the company would stay creative if younger executives were in charge.

In 1982 the Honda Motor Company opened the first Japanese car factory in the United States, in Marysville, Ohio. At first many Americans were not happy that a foreign-owned car factory had been built in their country. In protest, some people slashed the tires of Honda cars. As the company opened more plants, bringing good jobs and money to economically struggling towns and cities, Americans changed their minds.

Honda remained a director of the company for many years but also took time to enjoy his retirement. He especially liked hang gliding, playing golf, painting, and watching television on a set he installed in his bedroom ceiling.

He died on August 5, 1991, at the age of eighty-four.

Soichiro Honda left the world a unique manufacturing empire. In 2016 the Honda Motor Company sold about 4.7 million automobiles and 17 million motorcycles world-wide. Among its vast range of products, the company makes hybrid cars that help protect the environment because they run on electricity as well as gasoline, and small jets that operate as air taxis.

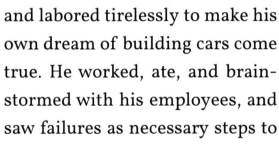

Soichiro Honda was an inventor with a passion for new ideas and improvements. He believed in the power of dreams and labored tirelessly to make his own dream of building cars come true. He worked, ate, and brainstormed with his employees, and saw failures as necessary steps to success. Because he broke with tradition and preferred new ways of doing things, Soichiro Honda is regarded as one of the world's pioneering businessmen.

Many people today may never have heard of Soichiro Honda, but almost everyone knows his last name!

TIMELINE

1906 November 17: Soichiro Honda was born in Komyo, Japan (now known as Tenryu).

1922 Moved to Tokyo to work in a garage. Trained for six years.

1928 Moved to Hamamatsu and opened a garage.

1935 Married Sachi Honda.

1936 Designed race cars and became Japan's racing champion.

1940 Perfected design for piston rings and sold them to Toyota. Began manufacturing propellers for Japanese air force for World War II.

1945 World War II ended. Honda designed a small motorcycle.

1948 Opened Honda Motor Company with business partner, Takeo Fujisawa.

1959 Introduced Super Cub motorcycles to the United States.

1969 Started shipping midsized cars to the United States.

1973 The Honda Civic arrived in the United States. Honda retired as president of the Honda Motor Company.

1991 August 5: Died at the age of eighty-four.

MORE WISDOM FROM
SOICHIRO HONDA

"A man shouldn't be measured by his height, but by his actions and the imprint he leaves on the history of mankind."

"I learned that the miracle laid in my willpower and repeated attempts. Believing deeply in something allows all of us to find tremendous inner strength and to surpass our limitations."

"I concluded that it wasn't necessary to be born rich or noble to succeed in life. Other qualities also entitle you to success: courage, perseverance, and ambitions."

"When I take temporary stock of my life, I measure how important contacts are, how this is worth more than all machine inventions because meeting people allows us to expand our vision of things, and get thousands of different experiences that we would never have had otherwise."

GLOSSARY

Allies (AL-eyes) *proper noun* the nations that fought Germany, Italy, and Japan in World War II, including the United States, the Soviet Union, the United Kingdom, and China as well as many others

atom (AH-tum) *noun* the smallest possible quantity of any substance

capitalist society (KA-puh-tuh-list so-SIGH-et-tee) *noun* a society with an economic system in which the production of goods is handled by private companies and the goods are sold to make a profit

carburetor (kar-bur-EH-tur) *noun* the part of a gasoline engine in which gasoline and air are mixed. When the mixture is burned, it provides the engine with power

combustible (kom-BUS-tuh-bull) *adjective* able to burn easily

conglomerate (kon-GLOM-er-ate) *noun* a company made up of many smaller businesses

conquer (KON-ker) *verb* to get the better of or take control

embargo (em-BAR-go) *noun* an official order that restricts trade between certain countries

emission standards (ee-MIH-shun STAN-durds) *noun* the limits on the quantity of air pollutants that a vehicle, factory, or other source can emit in a certain time frame, set by the government or another organization

emit (ee-MITT) *verb* to release or give off

engineer (EN-jin-eer) *noun* a person who designs and builds machines

executive (eks-EK-you-tiv) *adjective* relating to the management or direction of a company or the government; *noun* a person in charge of a company

ignite (IG-nite) *verb* to set on fire

innovation (EN-no-vay-shun) *noun* a new idea or way to do something

leverage (LEV-er-idge) *noun* influence used to gain an advantage

machinery (muh-SHEEN-air-ee) *noun* machines or parts of machines

manufacture (man-you-FAK-shure) *verb* to make a product, particularly in large quantities

mechanic (meh-KAN-ik) *noun* a person who fixes machines

mileage (MY-lij) *noun* number of miles traveled

nuclear (NEW-klee-ur) *adjective* of or relating to the energy created when the nuclei of atoms are combined or split apart

nucleus (NEW-klee-us) *noun* the central mass of an atom; *plural* nuclei

quadruple (kwa-DREW-pull) *verb* to become four times greater in number

smog (SMAHG) *noun* pollution made up of fog and smoke produced by cars and factories

slogan (SLOW-gun) *noun* a short phrase used by a company or team to attract attention

standardizing (STAND-er-DIE-zing) *verb* to change how things are done so that they are similar and consistent

tiller (TIL-ler) *noun* a handle that is used for steering

unconditional (un-kun-DISH-un-al) *adjective* without limits, absolute

viable (VI-a-bull) *adjective* workable

World War II (WURLD WOR TOO) *proper noun* a conflict involving more than thirty countries from 1939 to 1945, fought mainly in Europe, North Africa, Asia, and the South Pacific

TEXT SOURCES

Ager, Joseph. *Business or Pleasures*. Bloomington: iUniverse, 2006.

American Honda Motor Co., Ltd. https://www.honda.com/

Brain, Marshall "How Car Engines Work." *How Stuff Works*. Accessed February 9, 2018. https://auto.howstuffworks.com/engine2.htm

Cameron, Kevin. "Soichiro's Ladder: Twenty-five Years of Technical Progress." *Cycle*, September 1985.

Gelsanliter, David. *Jump Start: Japan Comes to the Heartland*. New York: Kodansha USA, 1992. First published 1990 by Hill and Wang.

Gibney, Frank. *Miracle by Design: The Real Reasons Behind Japan's Economic Success*. New York: Times Books, 1982.

Gregory, Fred M. H. "What Makes Honda Run?" *Town and Country*, March 1985.

Kamioka, Kazuyoshi. *Japanese Business Pioneers*. Union City, CA: Heian International, 1988.

Mair, Andrew. *Honda's Global Local Corporation*. New York: St. Martin's Press, 1994.

Miller, Karen Lowry. "A Car is Born." *Business Week*, September 13, 1993.

Mito, Setsuo. *The Honda Book of Management*. Atlantic Highlands, NJ: The Athlone Press, 1990.

Sakiya, Tetsuo. *Honda Motor: The Men, the Management, the Machines*. New York: Kodansha International, 1987.

Sanders, Sol W. *Honda: The Man and His Machine*. Boston: Little, Brown, 1975.

Satoru, Otsuki. *Good Mileage: The High-Performance Business Philosophy of Soichiro Honda*. Tokyo: NHK Publishing, 1996.

Schapp, John B. "Tycoon-San: The iconoclastic philosophy of Soichiro Honda." *Car and Driver*, June 1982.

Shook, Robert L. *Honda: An American Success Story*. New York: Prentice Hall, 1988.

Stokes, Henry Scott. "Market Guzzler." *Fortune*, February 20, 1984.

Statista: The Statistics Portal. "Worldwide number of automobiles sold by Honda Group from FY 2002 to FY 2017 (in 1,000s)." Accessed August 30, 2017. https://www.statista.com/statistics/267276/worldwide-automobile-sales-of-honda

Troy, Stewart. "The Americanization of Honda." *Business Week*, April 25, 1988.

SIDEBAR SOURCES

CARS: A BRIEF HISTORY

AutomoStory. "First Japanese Car." Accessed November 8, 2017. http://www.automostory.com/first-japanese-car.htm

Chaline, Eric. *Fifty Machines that Changed the Course of History*. Buffalo: Firefly Books, 2012.

Encyclopedia Japan. "Japanese Cars." Accessed September 17, 2017. https://doyouknowjapan.com/cars/

Ford Motor Company. "Our Story." Accessed November 8, 2017. https://corporate.ford.com/history.html

History.com. "This Day in History: Henry Ford test-drives his 'Quadricycle.'" Accessed November 8, 2017. http://www.history.com/this-day-in-history/henry-ford-test-drives-his-quadricycle

Kirsch, David A. *The Electric Vehicle and the Burden of History*. New Brunswick: Rutgers University Press, 2000.

Morris, Eric. "From Horse Power to Horsepower." *Access Magazine*, no. 30 (2007). https://www.accessmagazine.org/spring-2007/horse-power-horsepower/

STREET RACING IN JAPAN

McElroy, Ryan. "Midnight Club: Inside Japan's Most Infamous Illegal Street Racing Gang." *Car Keys.* Posted May 8, 2017. https://www.carkeys.co.uk/news/midnight-club-inside-japan-s-most-infamous-illegal-street-racing-gang

Garrett, Mike. "Kanjo Tribe: Osaka Night Fighters." *Speedhunters.* Posted February 27, 2013. http://www.speedhunters.com/2013/02/kanjo-tribe-osaka-night-fighters/

Honda Worldwide. "About Honda: A Neverending Passion for Racing." Accessed September 19, 2017. http://world.honda.com/history/challenge/07_racing/index.html

JAPAN IN WORLD WAR II

Atomic Heritage Foundation. "Atomic Timeline." Accessed November 30, 2017. https://www.atomicheritage.org/history/timeline

Atkins, Laura, and Stan Yogi. *Fred Korematsu Speaks Up.* Illustrated by Yutaka Houlette. Berkeley: Heyday, 2017.

Hall, Michelle. "By the Numbers: World War II's atomic bombs." CNN. Last updated August 6, 2013. http://www.cnn.com/2013/08/06/world/asia/btn-atomic-bombs/index.html

History.com. "Bombing of Hiroshima and Nagasaki." Accessed September 18, 2017. http://www.history.com/topics/world-war-ii/bombing-of-hiroshima-and-nagasaki

History.com. "Hirohito." Accessed September 18, 2017. http://www.history.com/topics/world-war-ii/hirohito

The National WWII Museum. "The Path to Pearl Harbor." Accessed November 8, 2017. https://www.nationalww2museum.org/war/articles/path-pearl-harbor

Office of the Historian. "Occupation and Reconstruction of Japan 1945-52." US Department of State. Accessed November 8, 2017. https://history.state.gov/milestones/1945-1952/japan-reconstruction

Schweber, S. S. *In the Shadow of the Bomb: Oppenheimer, Bethe, and the Moral Responsibility of the Scientist.* Princeton: Princeton University Press, 2000.

United Nations Treaty Collection. "No. 1832. Treaty of Peace with Japan. Signed at San Francisco, on 8 September 1951." Accessed November 29, 2017. https://treaties.un.org/doc/publication/unts/volume%20136/volume-136-i-1832-english.pdf

HENRY FORD AND THE ASSEMBLY LINE

CarHistory4u. "History of Motor Car: Automobile Production 1900–2003." Accessed September 20, 2017. http://www.carhistory4u.com/the-last-100-years/car-production (site discontinued)

History.com. "This Day in History: Ford's Assembly Line Starts Rolling." Accessed September 20, 2017. http://www.history.com/this-day-in-history/fords-assembly-line-starts-rolling

Swan, Tony. "Ford's Assembly Line Turns 100: How It Really Put the World on Wheels." *Car and Driver.* Posted April 2013. https://www.caranddriver.com/features/fords-assembly-line-turns-100-how-it-really-put-the-world-on-wheels-feature

HOW TO COOL AN ENGINE

New World Encyclopedia. "Internal Combustion Engine." Last updated April 18, 2014. http://www.newworldencyclopedia.org/entry/Internal_combustion_engine

Ofria, Charles. "A Short Course on Cooling Systems." *CarParts.* Last updated 2017. http://www.carparts.com/classroom/coolingsystem.htm

Parker, Barry. *The Isaac Newton School of Driving: Physics & Your Car.* Baltimore: John Hopkins University Press, 2003.

Safford, Jay. "What Is the Difference Between a Water-Cooled Engine and an Air-Cooled Engine?" *Your Mechanic.* Posted December 1, 2015. https://www.yourmechanic.com/article/what-is-the-difference-between-a-water-cooled-engine-and-an-air-cooled-engine

THE CLEAN AIR ACT AND THE ENERGY CRISIS

Ahlers, Christopher D. "Origins of the Clean Air Act: a New Interpretation." *Environmental Law* 45, no. 1 (2016). Accessed September 20, 2017. http://elawreview.org/articles/origins-of-the-clean-air-act-a-new-interpretation/

EPA. "Clean Air Act Requirements and History." Accessed September 20, 2017. https://www.epa.gov/clean-air-act-overview/clean-air-act-requirements-and-history

History.com. "Energy Crisis (1970s)." Accessed September 20, 2017. http://www.history.com/topics/energy-crisis

Office of the Historian. "Oil Embargo, 1973-1974." US Department of State. Accessed September 17, 2017. https://history.state.gov/milestones/1969-1976/oil-embargo

RECOMMENDED FURTHER READING

Fiction books are marked with an asterisk.

JAPAN

Buckley, A. M. *Japan*. Countries of the World. North Mankato, MN: Essential Library/ABDO, 2011.

Inzer, Christine Marie. *Diary of a Tokyo Teen: A Japanese-American Girl Travels to the Land of Trendy Fashion, High-Tech Toilets and Maid Cafes*. Clarendon, VT: Tuttle, 2016.

* Maetani, Vaelynn. *Ink and Ashes*. New York: Tu Books/ Lee & Low, 2015.

* Otowa, Rebecca. *My Awesome Japan Adventure: A Diary about the Best 4 Months Ever!* Clarendon, VT: Tuttle, 2013.

* Yumoto, Kazumi, trans. by Cathy Hirano. *The Friends*. New York: Farrar, Straus and Giroux Books for Young Readers, 1997.

CARS

Car: The Definitive Visual History of the Automobile. New York: Dorling Kindersley, 2011.

Hammond, Richard. *Car Science*. New York: Dorling Kindersley, 2008.

Newton, Tom. *How Cars Work*. Vallejo, CA: Black Apple Press, 1999.

Watts, Pam. *Gasoline Engines*. Mendota Heights, MN: North Star Editions Inc., 2017.

ENGINEERING AND ENGINEERS

Burgan, Michael. *Who Was Henry Ford?* Who Was. New York: Grosset & Dunlap, 2014.

Ignotofsky, Rachel. *Women in Science: 50 Fearless Pioneers Who Changed the World*. New York: Penguin Random House, 2016.

Morgan, George D. *Rocket Girl: The Story of Mary Sherman Morgan, America's First Female Rocket Scientist*. Amherst, NY: Prometheus Books, 2013.

Popular Mechanics Co. *Projects for the Young Mechanic: Over 250 Classic Instructions & Plans*. New York: Dover Publications, 2013.

Shetterly, Margot Lee. *Hidden Figures*. Young Readers' Edition. New York: HarperCollins Children's Books, 2016.

WORLD WAR II

Bradley, James, with Ron Powers. *Flags of Our Fathers.* Young Readers' Edition. Adapted by Michael French. New York: Delacorte Books for Young Readers, 2001.

* Bruchac, Joe. *Code Talker: A Novel about the Navajo Marines of World War Two.* New York: Dial Books for Young Readers, 2005.

* Coerr, Eleanor. *Sadako and the Thousand Paper Cranes.* New York: G. P. Putnam's Sons, 1977.

Demuth, Patricia Brennan. *What Was Pearl Harbor?* What Was. New York: Grosset & Dunlap, 2013

Panchyk, Richard. *World War II for Kids: A History with 21 Activities.* Chicago: Chicago Review Press, 2002.

Sheinkin, Steve. *Bomb: The Race to Build—and Steal—the World's Most Dangerous Weapon.* New York: Flash Point, 2012.

ABOUT THE AUTHOR AND ILLUSTRATOR

MARK WESTON's inspiration for this children's book about Soichiro Honda came from the extensive research he did for his highly praised adult book about pioneering men and women of Japan, called *Giants of Japan*. A former attorney, journalist, and *Jeopardy!* contestant, Weston is now a full-time writer. He lives in Armonk, New York.

KATIE YAMASAKI is an illustrator, author, muralist, fine artist, and teaching artist. Growing up in the "car culture" of Detroit, Yamasaki had an immediate connection to Honda's story. Yamasaki comes from a huge, diverse family that is full of (among many other things) artists and teachers. She lives in Brooklyn, New York. You can visit Katie online at katieyamasaki.com.